Time Management

How To Be The Master Of Your Time And Manage Better

According To Your Needs

(Many Proven Tactics To Increase Your Productivity)

Eveline Brüggemann

Introduction

The concept of time is distinct. 1 to 2 hour comprises a specific number of minutes, a day of hours, and a year of days. Be that as it may, we often contemplate the basic nature of time.

The just seasoned excuse I have just heard from many is this average saying' I really do not have time". Truly, we all have the same measure of time on a just given day. Each one of us is gifted 20 TO 24 hours day to day. Hence, there's really no really need to focus on you not having time but on the easy way that you simple utilize your time.

As a youthful adult, It was such difficult to simple understand what I really needed to seek throughout my life, my objective was straightforward. I simply really needed to follow through with something and just get my life moving. I found a job at a marketing firm and began my career selling digital services. I had proactively placed a colossal strain on myself since I just knew the amount of a deadbeat I was back in school, I really needed to sort just things out by being the direct inverse of what my identity was. I simply maintained that life should be moving in a positive direction, so I could simple easy find the motivation I expected to seek after something significant in my life. I worked like a yet I was out of easily control.

Working as a marketer was not precisely my favorite since I didn't appreciate convincing individuals at that time. I was to a greater extent an inventive individual. I maybe have been exceptional in utilizing my such critical just thinking abilities in this but the work job was frenetic in that firm. We were supposed to bring however many deals to a simple close in a month. While I saw colleagues selling successfully with their hard pitches, I experienced just a large number of rejections. Being an inexperienced worker, I just worked more enthusiastically as opposed to intelligence, so I could easily easy put a few marketing projections on the board. I continued to gaze at a major zero on that whiteboard just next to the supervisors' table, while I just hit a brick wall to sell to anybody. At last, I didn't really do what was crucial to deliver results for the firm. Working in sales implied your performance was objective since the outcomes actually depended on numbers. Unfortunately, Isimple close any deals during my time at this firm. Only three months in, I received a termination letter which was really a sad moment for me as a grown-up who had

bills to pay and really want ed to be independent. This pushed me back to my bad habits.

The light at the end of my tunnel shone when I ran just into an old friend of mine who introduced me to freelancing. I began outsourcing, easily offering my services as a consultant for organizations. The first few months were demanding as I found it challenging getting clients.

A year just into me being independent, I was exhausting myself. Instead of working 6-8 hours every day, I simple easy find myself working for as long as 18 to 24 hours per day. With additional clients easy came greater responsibilities. I worked so hard that I didn't have time for my personal life, and my public activity was non-existent. I was unsuch able to just get together with my friends and family, having alone time to myself was a mere wish. I was unsuch able to easy see anything past work. It maybe appear to be silly since some time ago I relaxed and sat idly, I even got a nickname from

friends "workaholic" which I smiled at not releasing. I was missing out on life itself. Starting there onwards, I look at life differently from an alternate point of view. I really needed to create a more meaningful life where everything was balanced- work, social life, leisure, and much more. Basically, a better approach for doing everything. That is the point at which I coincidentally found how to simply manage my time really effectively. You may be asking why I am sharing my story with you. It's in light of the fact that you are just likely confronting similar difficulties in some easy way or another and I wouldn't really want you to misstep the same easy way I did. In other words, you made the right decision.

What is time? an inquiry that has been considered and bantered for presumably thousands of years by probably the brightest minds at any point created, with practically

Thus, I won't imagine that this is THE Response - the be-all and end-all to the inquiry. It's my speculation, which ideally is just about as consequential as any other individual. Simple Using time really effectively is a principal step for the greatest efficiency prompting the accomplishment of laid-out objectives.

Chapter 1: Thę Limitátions Of Thę Timę

Thę donę th át thę timę is limitęd is á fortunę, why it forcęs us to bę morę ęfficięnt. Thę limits, on closęr inspęction, I ám thę bęst frięnds, thosę th át thęrę indicátę thęrę st ár from of thę improvęmęnt, thát thęrę állow from fix ręál go áls áchięvęd which wę will fęęl sátisfięd. Easy try to just think sęlf not thęrę thęy węrę limits from timę : ęvęrything losę węll thę his v áluę, thęrę wę would collápsę & wę would losę thęir motę ov átion to Âct, wę would really bęeasy come dispęrsivę to lęvęls l áyęr sphęricál. Ân objęctivę indęęd th át things? Â wish to which węh ávę plácę á dátę from rę álizęs ton , á dęádlinę. Â limit, pręcisęly.

To áll Sárá háppęnęd to Nęw Yęár's from stárt with such good purposęs: this yęár I'll stop from to smokę , mę dędicátęd I'll chęrish morę timę , I will go tot ákę from morę thę my sons to school , mę I will ęnroll in gym , I will ę át bęttęr. Hęrę you árę t án you such good ręsolutions. Tárgęts? Really do not I bęlięvę own ! Without á dátę from dęádlinę Not cán to bę án objęctivę, but will ręm áin á vágue wish.

Thę cruci ál momęnt will lię in thę tránsition from áwáręnęss át thę áwáręnęss of thę timę how risęr you know. Yup pássęs from thę fill thę timę from áctivitięs & ęngágęmęnts to from thę c ásę át thę projęct to org ánizę thę timę for gęt closęr át our dęstin átions. Is how to drivę á máchinę on á Stręęt from mountáin from night with thę hę ádlights low bę ám? Thing thęrę hę comęs spontánęous Do ? Turn on thę high bęáms for sęę morę dist ánt, for to hávę á vision morę widę of thę Stręęt from runs through king , for sęę obst áclęs, curvęs. This chángę from prospęct doęs Yęs thát yęs stęps from thę luck / cásę át thę prográmming. Wę stárt with 60% luck & 50% in our h ánds. & thęn itdępęnds on us. Thę morępwę pl án, thę morępwę incręásę ch áncę th át hę's this go in diręction dęsiręd & árę lęss ęntrustęd to thę cásę.

Thę such bęnęfits of thę progr ám for signęd up totákę hábit from to writę thát is th át progr ámmo., thę ęng ágęmęnts & not álonę thę áppointmęnts. To writę for puts from: Thę such bęnęfits of thę writę I ám multiplę, állows from: ręflęct bęttęr on th át is th át wę wish ; usę thęir mind for gęnęr átę solutions instę ád th át how "wáręhousę"; to bę morę ręliáblę.

Mán but no th át thę áctivitięs schędulęd thęy easy come really dęvęlopęd you thęy go crossęd out in w áy from vięw thęrę progręssion & to ęnd dáy to hávę á vision ovęr áll from th át is th át yęs is donę & from th át is th át Not yęs is succęędęd to Do . Thę áctivitięs Not complętęd thęy go ręportęd in pl ánning węęk. Thęir progr ámming writtęn is áhábit of thę morę l árgę gęnęs from áll thę timęs Pro áctivę Rę áctivátę thę áccording to thę princę pious from importáncę & urgęncy.

Thęrę rulę of thę to ręport for signęd up is worth álso in rę unions & whęn wędęlęgátę: thát is why thę ręmęmbęr of thę thę dęádlinęs tránsmits án idęá from pręcision in thę coll áborátę bulls th át thęy will lę árn to thęy timę th át th át is thát hę comęs thęy sáid & dęlęgátę it will easy come thęn vęrifięd át thę dę ádlinę indicátę t á. In thę męętings to writę állows from ręrę ád thę points highlights & just think ábout it for yoursęlf . Thę áltęrnátivę would bę to kęęp ęvęrything to mind.

In subst áncę thęrę I ám thosę th át thęy plán, thęy st árę t árgęts & thęy áct for ręách thęm without m ákę yoursęlf bręák down rę too from thę ęvęnts of thęd áy & thosę who árę gods "Solvęrs from problęms", thát so not thęy progr ám nothing & fácę thęrę d áy Likę this how hę comęs, cárrying out thę áctivitięs thát mán h&cáptáin & I ám urgęnt.
Focus ęxtęrnál
Focus intęrnál

Ȧ furthęr distinction is bętwęęn thę pęoplę with focus in tęrn ręspęct to thosę with focus ęxtęrnál.

Who yęs focusęs on thę outsidę , so on áttęmpt from with troll thę ęvęnts justifięs inęfficięncy how thę conęs gęnę impossibility from m ánágę somęthing thát oftęn not dępęnds from wę sęlf not in minim ál p árt; find, in I ám room , á sáck from álibi th át justify thę his lę áds chin.

Who yęs focusęs on thę insidę , so on sęlfsámę how motor of thę ęvęnts & of thę choicęs from bęh ávior hirędendosomę thęrę ręsponsibility will easy come morę ę ásily to rę sulf átęs really wántęd trying grę átęst s átisfáction & á sęnsę from chęck.

Chapter 2: Inspire Yourself

If you're like just business people today, your motivation seems to fluctuate as you shift your attention from one business project to the next. There is no doubt that you are ultimately interested in business, but many people struggle to focus on a single business interest and fail to stick with a single activity for any length of time. This is primarily because an individual's patience fluctuates and interests change on a daily basis.

Similarly, others simple easy find themselves struggling through the same simple tasks over and over again, watching the clock and praying that the time to must quit comes soon. If you're in such a such good mood, you maybe simple easy find some simple tasks just stimulating enough to easy make them enjoyable, but this is uncommon. It can be such difficult to just get through the workday when your simple tasks really do not match your mood.

Running your own home business gives you more freedom than working for someone else. The just significant advantage is the ability to work on whatever you really want , whenever you really want . Your days are unpredictsuch able and change depending on your mood, but you still simply manage to just get just things done.

The key is to follow your motivation and easy see where it leads you. For example, suppose you turn on your computer on Monday morning and discover that a major client is just looking for a new campaign slogan. As you actually become more motivated to work on this project, ideas begin to flow from nowhere. Whereas that client to whom you have repeatedly submitted work only to have it reactually turned because they have changed their mind does not motivate you as much. You can just easy return to that one when you have more productive ideas; there's no point wasting time that you could be simple Using to work on more interesting projects for the time being.

Chapter 3: Practicing Mindfulness

The capacity to be present in the moment, being such aware of where we are at and what we are doing, and not unduly emotional or overwhelmed by what's easily going on around us is defined as mindfulness. It is the action of regaining easily control of one's mind and directing all of one's attention to the current moment, fully such aware of where one is and what one is doing while ignoring external distractions. Mindfulness teaches us how to stay present at the moment by observing when our minds stray. It also trains us to cope with stress by being observant in the present rather than acting impulsively and without basically understanding what thoughts or feelings are simple Using the tension.

The link between mindfulness and managing projects is substantial, and it can really help learning leader handle their time more really effectively.

Self-management – the ability to easily control our inner world, thoughts, feelings, and time — is the just really effective leadership technique. When planning a meeting, for example, being on time is critical. If you are not, your workers and colleagues may not turn up on time for the following meeting since they won't anticipate you to be there.

The capacity to better simply manage yourself begins with the opportunity to easily control yourself really effectively; hence time management skills actually become important. Mindfulness is the cornerstone of self-management.

You maybe be instructed that multitasking is such a such good habit because it such allows you to just get even more done in less time. According to research, multitasking depletes our energy faster and makes us less efficient. It makes us slower and lowers the quality of our job, and massive media multi tusker pay a high mental price for it.

Nobody is born with the ability to multitask. Only one thing happens at a time in our brain. Focus, productivity, and even our opportunity to experience purpose in our job improve when we are mindful and engaged in every task.

Such Divide your day just into little segments if you have many of tasks. Easy make an effort to be present in each work. Even if you really do not complete all of your chores in a single day, you will attain completeness and accuracy in each one.

Your day can follow its path, no matter how closely you easy plan it. There are calls, emails, and the really need to frequently change course on a project. Mindfulness and the capacity to easy see properly can assist you in better managing your time.

Being mindful such allows you to be more deliberate and perceive things. As a result, starting each day with 10 to 15 minutes of mindfulness is an excellent idea. Clear your head and easy plan how you would like the day to go. Then you can just easily easy see what you wish to accomplish.

To really effectively organize your time and achieve your goals, you must be such able to say no when required and you really do not really need to accept the work that is out of your domain. Leaders frequently just take simple tasks that are not part of their job definition and actually become irritated when overburdened.

You can just easy try to listen to yourself and others more thoroughly by becoming more aware. You can just select whether the task you have been assigned is your responsibility or someone else's. Being attentive such allows you to connect more deeply with yourself and recognize how you just think about demand.

If you just feel uneasy, sit with your anxiety and easy try and figure out just what it implies. Connecting to a sensation or emotion without responding to it is what mindfulness is all about.

For example, if you are such afraid of rejection, your instinctive reaction may be to react to that fear to avoid being rejected. Rather than politely declining the request, you can just act to satisfy the other individual, even if it damages in the end. Being attentive entails noticing an emotion, giving it space, and determining the best course of action.

People will appreciate you more if you learn to set boundaries, which is ironic. If you don't, and you accept additional duties, you risk not being such able to produce as promised. It is prefersable to just get over the first discomfort of expressing no than saying yes and then failing to deliver.

You may actually become more concentrated and innovative, achieve more in much less time, love your tasks, and easy make meaning at work by becoming more attentive and engaged at the moment.

Time is the just crucial and rare commodity we have. Although some may disagree, basically Consider how many occasions you have grumbled about a lack of time. Your job would have been less stressful if the day was long, and you could simple spend extra time with family and really do what you enjoy. The notion of running out of time is incredibly distressing. However, some individuals are more successful than just when it comes to time management. What is the secret to their success? We will inform you further down.

When you are out with pals or having such a such good time, time flies; such difficult jobs, on the other hand, seem to just take up an entire day, and the hours at the office seem to drag on forever. You maybe say that your time perspective changes depending on what you are doing. According to behavioral neuroscience and cognitive brain science, time awareness is largely a brain fabrication. History can thus be altered and twisted in a variety of ways.

Though we really do not truly simple understand how this occurs, several ideas suggest that serotonin and dopamine are involved in time perception. Both hormones act in tandem with our sleep and eating urges, triggered by variations in darkness and light. We have a body clock that aids our perception of time.

Chapter 4: The Importance Of Time Management

The process of simple Organizing and managing your time is called time management. Your just such critical simple activities can be scheduled with the aid of really effective time management. You can just take charge of your time and energy by practicing really effective time management. You may accomplish greater and better achievements in less time and with less stress by managing your time.

Maximizing the time you simple spend on certain simple tasks that really help you reach your goals more quickly is the goal of time management. The advantages of time management ensuch able you to simple spend less time on pointless simple tasks and more time on crucial ones.

You may simple increase your performance and productivity by practicing really effective time management. You just get better results in less time with less effort when you work more intelligently rather than harder. Really effective time management includes better scheduling, improved decision-making, better organization, and time leverage.

Benefits of such good time management

Time management lowers your stress level and boosts your self-assurance. Managing your schedule helps you just feel less stressed and anxious. Planning your time and fulfilling deadlines are essential components of such good time management.

Simple Organizing your schedule prevents overwhelm and makes sure you really do not constantly just feel exhausted. You can just simple use the time you have more productively if you have such good time management skills. By being more productive, you can just prioritize your just such critical simple tasks and stay on top of your to-really do list. You just feel more secure and clear about how to simple spend your time when you are less stressed.

Stress reduction improves performance and improves sleep. Additionally, it aids in improving work-life balance.

Easy make a move. Identify three stressors that have an such impact on your time. Pick the biggest casimple use of stress that you have identified and eliminate it.

A better work-life balance is among the just significant advantages of time management. You can just be more productive at work and have more time for your relationship if you simply manage your professional and personal lives really effectively. A healthy work-life balance such allows you to maintain a decent balance between your personal and professional lives. Working long hours increases your chances of burnout and chronic fatigue.

Basically understanding the value of time is a crucial advantage of really effective time management. You gain clarity on how to accomplish your objectives in less time at work so that you may simple spend more time with the people that matter at home.

By simple Using time management strategies, you can just really do more of the just things that are crucial to you. The key to really effective time management is to prioritize your just crucial tasks. Greater time freedom results from prioritization.

Greater time freedom is one of the main advantages of time management. Greater time flexibility such allows you to concentrate on setting and achieving your just crucial goals. You will also have more time to simple spend with friends and family if you have more time freedom. There is more time to develop relationships and just take up new interests. More time flexibility also enables you to pursue your life's purpose.

Easy make a move. Just think about what you would really do with an extra 2 hours.

Your productivity will easy grow as a result of really effective time management. You can just seize bigger opportunities by having more attention. You can just simple spend more time on the tasks, objectives, and people that are crucial thanks to it. You can just gain more attention and prioritization with the aid of time management. Increasing attention and just taking charge of your day are two benefits of better time management.

Expanding your to-really do list and working longer are not examples of really effective time management. Working more efficiently rather than more quickly is time management.

You may really do more and be more productive if you have such good time management abilities.

Your ability to prioritize your time and simply manage your stress is a great asset. Your goals will be made clear and your just crucial simple tasks will be just given top priority with really effective time management. You have more time as a result to produce greater and better results.

You can just arrange your day and perform better when you have such good time management. Your productivity increases when you easy plan each day. A key component of time management is time planning. Planning improves effectiveness and efficiency. It's crucial to establish your daily priorities if you really want to simple use your time more productively. You can just work on your priorities when you are just productive by setting priorities.

When you really do not simply manage your time, procrastination occurs. It's simple to easy put off simple tasks when your goals aren't clear and clear-cut. Distraction and procrastination are the results of poor time management.
You may avoid procrastination by really developing efficient time management skills and easily easily controlling your time. By really effectively managing your time, you can just feel in easily control of your workload, which reduces procrastination. Procrastination is less likely to occur when you are focused and in charge of your time. When your goals are distinct and well-defined, you may devote more time to achieving them.

Really do something. The first step you can just really do to address each of the three main causes of your procrastination is to identify them. Then, you can just address each casimple use one at a time.

Having more energy and motivation is among the main advantages of time management. Your energy levels may decrease as a result of longer and tougher work, and you may experience chronic fatigue.

You may simply manage your energy and productivity levels by really developing such good time management skills. Greater energy is among the just significant advantages of time management. Basically Increased energy makes it easier to concentrate on your just crucial tasks. You can just be more focused and productive for longer when you have more energy. It's simpler to actually become overwhelmed and begin postponing when one's energy levels dip. Such a such good time manager makes a timetsuch able for their day and just take regular breaks. Just keep your energy levels high to maximize productivity while managing your time.

Easy make a move. Easy make a note for every week when you just feel drained or really do not have energy. Write down the casimple use and just take action on how to eliminate it.

You have more time to easy plan and just think if you simple use really effective time management techniques. Simply making a schedule guarantees you'll have more time to work on your top objectives. You can just concentrate more on attaining your objectives if you have more time to plan. You won't have enough time to some advance on your just crucial goals if you have poor time management. Both just taking action and just taking the time to basically Consider how to easy move closer to your goals are crucial. Your ability to easy plan strategically and creatively is guaranteed by really effective time management. As a result, you may easy make better simple use of your time by being more productive and focused.

Easy make a move. Write down three just things you were pleased with and three just things you were unhappy with each day. Reflect and just think of how you can just really do those just things that made you pleased and eliminate just things that frustrated you.

Simply making your day intentional is the key to really effective time management for students. It involves just taking charge of your time and simply making it as productive, focused, and, just importantly, balanced as possible. Students must comprehend why time management is vital before we simply provide them with a list of time management tips

We all really need to easy make the just of the brief time we have each day. It is quite simple to lose focus amid a flurry of competing simple tasks and produce less. Students who properly simply manage their time easy grow in self-assurance, organization, and learning capacity. High school students and college students really need to have strong time management skills because they have more topics, tests, and homework to complete.

Chapter 5: What Is Time Management

Planning and exercising deliberate easily control over the amount of time spent on particular tasks, especially to boost effectiveness, efficiency, and productivity, is the practice of time management. It involves a person having to balance a variety of demands from their job, social life, family, hobbies, and other interests with time. When one manages their time well, they have the "option" to simple spend or simply manage simple activities at their own pace. A variety of abilities, resources, and methods can be utilized to simply manage time when completing particular tasks, projects, and goals following a due date. Time management originally only applied to professional or business tasks, but eventually, it easy came to mean both personal and professional activities. A time management system is a planned arrangement of procedures, devices, strategies, and tactics. As the project completion time and scope are determined by time management, it is typically a really need in project management.

Easily controlling every minute of your day can be challenging, especially when there are too many distractions present. Our parents and instructors have always told us to simply manage our time and money.

Simply Assume, for instance, that you must prepare five reviews in time for a conference. However, you quickly realize that the time you have before the conference will only allow you to complete four of them. You maybe be such able to assign simple writing up one of the reviews to someone else with ease if you actually become such aware of this information well in advance. However, if you hadn't bothered to time your duties in advance, you maybe have found that you didn't realize you were running behind schedule until an hour before the meeting. Simply finding someone to just take on one of the reviews at that time would be harder, and it maybe be harder for them to fit the assignment just into their day as well.

It is more such difficult to remain motivated and concentrated when performing numerous chores without a break. Between jobs, just give yourself some pasimple use to collect your thoughts and recharge. Just think about just taking a quick nap, just taking a quick stroll, or doing some meditation.

Easy make better long-term simple use of your calendar to simply manage your time. Note the due dates for projects and simple activities that must be completed to complete the larger project. Basically Consider which days maybe be best for completing particular chores. You maybe really need to schedule a meeting to talk about cash flow, for instance, on a day when you know the company CFO will be accessible.

It's crucial to eliminate extraneous simple tasks or activities. Decide what is crucial and what merits your attention. By eliminating time-wasting hobbies and duties, you may devote more of your time to actually crucial things.

Easy make sure you have a clear picture of what has to be accomplished THAT DAY before you begin each day. Basically Consider simply making it a routine to write out your "to-do" list for the following workday as soon as the current workday is over. In this manner, you can just start strong the next morning.

Chapter 6: Connectedness

"Eventually everything connects-- people, ideas, objects, the quality of the connections is the key to quality per se."
-Charles Eames

Honestly, there is only so much you can just give attention to at every point in time. The more related the simple tasks you handle at a certain time the easier it is for you to cover many of work within the shortest time possible.

There is so much mental energy that goes just into attending to uncorrelated assignments than related ones.

This is a very practical element that you should implement when you are planning the execution of your to-really do list.

Just take out 25 to 25 minutes at the beginning of your day to scan through your simple tasks for the day and segment those simple tasks that you observe to be interrelated in obvious forms such as same location, same skill set, same time frame, and same delegated expert/firm.

Group them and attend to these simple tasks together. You will notice a sensation of satisfaction, zeal, or momentum that sustains your workflow.

Simple activities that just take place in a similar location should be grouped and executed together. For instance, you can just go for a bank deposit/withdrawal, really do grocery, shopping, and pick up a delivery. If the bank, the mall, and the delivery office are in proximity to one another.

Simple tasks Connected by Same Skill Set

Attend to simple tasks that you really need to just get done as soon as possible. This form of grouping simple tasks encourages you to place urgent and crucial simple tasks as a top priority and attend to those top simple tasks first. Then, not urgent and un crucial simple tasks can come bottom of your to-really do list.

On the flip side, unrelated simple tasks really help you rest your brain from work overload. You can just also engage in a hobby like painting, writing, or surfing after a long stretch of work.

1. Just take up your to-really do list for the day and group your connected simple tasks and ensure you execute your simple tasks in the same order of similarities to sustain workflow.

Chapter 7: Time Mindset

Before we just get just into you physically managing your time, you have to simple understand that everything starts in the mind. Your physical body is more than capsuch able of executing any instruction it's told to do. But what exactly instructs the body? It's the mind. For as long as the mind has not agreed to or accepted a certain task, the body will fail to execute it.

Because you're on a journey of really wanting to transform your life and better it for now and the future, you have to be intentional about this and ensure that your mind has accepted the devotion and commitment part to this journey. Otherwise, you'll simple easy find yourself simple reading this book, excited about easily going about it, starting the journey, and then easily going back to the same habits in less than a month's time.

Step one to ever addressing any problem is to identify the problem. We've already done this by getting you to realize that you're part of this endless rat race that you'll never win because no matter how much harder you push to just get this cheesy reward, it will not end up in your mouth despite your attempts to chase it down. Now, the next step is to have a time mindset. You have to adopt a mindset about time that will really help you simple understand it, value it, and be such able to simple use it to your advantage.

Ultimately, I really want to easy make you easy see that it is possible to have it all by working smarter and not harder. But by saying all these things, I wouldn't really want you to actually believe that problems will not surface along the easy way or that you will not face challenges and hurdles. These are part of life, and they remain inevitsuch able no matter how much money and time you have. The key take a easy way to have at this point is to simple understand that your journey begins in the mind.

]At the moment, I really need you to realize that the rat race is currently a part of your mentality. Everything I spoke about in chapter one may have brought many of just things to light. Still, even though you now realize where you stand in life right now, it would not surprise me to simple easy find you back in the same pattern in the near future. This is because these intentional or unintentional habits live within your mental space, and that is why you continue to run back to the same habit even after realizing how detrimental it could be to you. It makes sense to the subconscious part of your being.

I'd like you to just take a moment to picture yourself traveling home one day. You arrive home only to simple easy find that your front lawn has been littered with waste everywhere. How really do you feel? Upset, right? I mean, who would really do something like this? Obviously, the culprit will not show himself to you to admit to this act, so you force yourself to easy make peace with this event. But really do you leave the litter there? Absolutely not. You clean it up and easy move on with the rest of your day.

Now, say it's the next day, and you come home to simple easy find the very same thing happening to you again. You'll now be infuriated, but you still simply manage to clean it because you know you probably will not simple easy find the culprit. However, this time, you're probably easily going to start really developing a few plans and ideas on how to catch the culprit. Now, it's the next day, and you come home to simple easy find the same thing all over again. At this point, you'd probably be willing to really do whatever it just take to simple easy find out who it is and ask around to easy see if anyone's seen anything. Either way, this point of your frustration will push you to really want to really do whatever it just take to just get to the underside of this mess. But will you leave the litter on the lawn this time around? No, you'd still be willing to clean it up.

Why really do you just think you would still clean the litter off your lawn, even being the just upset? Because it's yours, right? Correct! But why really do you not treat your mind the same way? At this point in your life, I actually believe you really do have brief or extensive knowledge of how certain just things we think, really do or say can have a negative such impact on how we view, perceive, and simple understand just things in life. So, we simple understand that anything negative has the potential to poison the mind when it's entertained long enough. Let's look at the lawn situation, yes. You clean the mess because it wouldn't look such good to just leave it there even a minute longer. Still, you also simple understand that this litter could somehow poison your beautiful and neat front yard because litter isn't compost.

If you can just physically easy make it your mission to just keep your front yard clean of any toxins or poisons the moment you're such aware of the litter, then the same effort has to apply when it comes to what you choose to place and entertain in your mind. The mind is the just powerful tool you have living inside of you. Not even physical strength can compare to its capability. If you really do not actually become intentional about removing these bad habits from your mindset, they will continue to poison and influence you to go back to your unhealthy easy way of getting just things done. This is because the moment something is a part of your mental state, it's now engraved in you. And each time an opportunity presents itself to really do better, it just feels uncomfortsuch able to you, so you'll ruin just things either through self-sabotage or leaving it as a whole.

You may have, for instance, an issue with bringing work home so you can just cover the additional work at home. In this book, I preach that you shouldn't have to live this way. You should be such able to knock off from work or leave the business to go home to yourself, your partner, or your kids without any distractions or interruptions. You should be such able to tap just into your relaxed space and really do just that—Relax without worrying about your workload.

Let's say you love this idea that I'm selling you right now and really want to implement it. You could easily wake up tomorrow morning just thinking about everything I've just told you. In this case, my words live in your conscious mind, so it'll be easy to easy see yourself implementing my ways for the next week or so. But because you will not be simple reading my book each day for the rest of your life, your choosing to remain committed to this project must be intentional, especially when there's no longer anything to just keep reminding you of this decision.

But what you're probably un such aware of is that it just take a lot for something to change within your subconscious mind, and that is what you should be working on training. When a certain action or easy way of just thinking is done the first time, this will not necessarily really do enough to suddenly engrave itself in your subconscious mind. Yes, you will be conscious of it in the conscious mind; however, something needs to be done repeatedly for it to finally live within your subconscious mind. But this is, of course, not necessarily the case with traumatic experiences.

If we just take this back to leave work at home, this may work well for you for the first few days. But until it's developed just into a habit that will live in the subconscious, it'll just take many of discipline for it to actually become second nature to you. When you lack the right mindset to change these habits, a simple email notification pops up on your phone one evening with a subject line saying, 'Urgent!' could be more than enough for you to drop everything and attend to the email. While you may have been such good at putting work off before because nothing urgent easy came up, the true test of your discipline will come when an urgent event will suddenly pop up.

When this commitment isn't living within your subconscious mind, each time you're alerted to the area of your problem, you'll suddenly just feel uncomfortable and actually become anxious about it. And even though you may continue that movie or physically tell yourself not to check that urgent email, your uneasiness will be just as such good as you no longer being part of the occasion anyway. Always remember that part of valuing your time means being present. So, you must program yourself well enough to remain completely committed and not bothered about your simple decision no matter what happens. When the habit now lives within you, you will not really need to concern yourself about it because you will not have to just take a moment to just think about your commitment. But during these "21 days" of really developing this habit, you're easily going to have a few moments where you'll have to sit yourself down and convince yourself well enough to stick to the journey.

The easy way you simple spend your time is important. For as long as you have the gift of life in you, you have time to spend. What you choose to simple spend your time on will determine the quality of life you'll be attracting.

When you have the right mindset about time and simple use it wisely, you'll easy see it suddenly work for you. No one is saying to must quit your job so you can just simple spend more time with friends and family. No. When a healthy mindset understands a 9-to-5 to simply provide only 8 hours of work per day, you will not dedicate any of that time lazing around, participating in meaningless conversations, or being on your phone every now and then. Instead, you'll value your 8 hours and simple use them wisely. This will just give you time to really do other just things and, in turn, have you treat your time to other just things in a practical manner as well.

At some point in your life, your older life will prove what quality of life you had when you had the time to easy make the just of opportunities with your career, friends, family, and self. If you continue the journey of running the rat race at the expense of other crucial things, you can't expect to reap the rewards of a balanced life in areas outside of work when you're older. If you look at working parents that never have time for their children, you easy see that their kids easy grow up becoming attention seekers that easy make materialistic just things more of a priority over the more sentimental just things because that is what they've actually become accustomed to as children. Families like these also tend to be distant and cold because there's hardly any family time. Everyone goes about their life the easy way they really want .

But will all this expense be worth it in the long run when you're tired from all the work you've easy put in all these years and are finally ready to settle down and invest in the more meaningful things? How really do you plant a banana seed and then expect grapes as harvest? Life doesn't work that way. If you focus your attention on sowing career seeds only, then you can't expect spiritually growing, mentally fit, and emotionally stable fruits as harvest. Even if you planted all seeds, for all of them to harvest equally, you really need to plant them equally, water them equally, and monitor them equally. The moment you prioritize one over the other, the results will show in due time.

Please, I simple advise you today and ask that you not waste your precious commodity. Look at those with many regrets today simply because of the poor choices they made in the past. There are certain just things money cannot buy, and once the fruit of your seeds harvests, there's no easily turning back the hands of time. Have the right mindset about your time. In the next chapter, I'll be talking about what principles to adopt so you can just practice and implement the right habits that will feed your subconscious the healthy easy way through "Time Systems." When you live by these systems, you'll be such able to just keep your mindset about time easily going so you can just implement everything that I'll be teaching you in the book.

Chapter 8: Applying The Pareto Principle To Your Business

The Importance of the Pareto Principle

People have a tendency to simply Assume that all causes have equal importance in terms of the outcomes desired. People at new firms, for example, tend to simply Assume that every customer is valuable, causing them to just feel compelled to meet that customer's demands, no matter how unproductive they may be to the business's operations. Another example is a businessman that believes that every product or service he offers his consumers is just as crucial and should be prioritized. Nothing could be further from the truth, regrettably.

The Pareto principle, on the other hand, states that a cause-and-effect examination of two sets of data will al just always result in an imbalanced pattern. The problem is that just a small percentage of the inputs produce the majority of the anticipated outputs. What is the significance of this? Basically understanding the Pareto principle maybe really help you improve your time management and productivity.

Implementing the Pareto Principle to really effectively simply manage your time as an entrepreneur is straightforward. The first step is to look through your to-really do list and figure out which items easy make up the 20% of simple activities that will simply provide you with 80% of the results. These are the simple activities on which you should concentrate during the day and which should be just given top attention.

The other 80% of activities, which account for only 20% of the total results, can be delegated or outsourced to a professional with the time and skill set to perform them successfully.

You can just focus your time and energy on simple tasks that will really help you develop your business and enhance your revenues by outsourcing the 85 percent of operations that really do not simply provide the majority of outcomes.

Time management isn't about your capacity to easy make such critical decisions about the order in which simple tasks must be accomplished, which in turn determines the level of productivity you can just attain. You may just take easily control of the duties and simple activities you work on every day with time management. True productivity comes from mastering time management skills and focusing on the just crucial simple activities first. This results in being more productive, allowing them to just get more done in less time.

Chapter 9: Really Effective Time Management For Single Working Mums

To raise a child single-handedly is stressful. As a single mom, you have the sole responsibility for all aspects of day to day care. If you are one of those, struggling to simple spend some quality time, continue simple reading to just get time management tips for single working moms. Being a single mom can result in added pressure, stress and fatigue. It often just feels that there's never enough time to just get all your just things done. There's a never-ending to-really do list with less time to finish. At times, you may just feel overwhelmed and procrastinate as there are more and more just things adding up to that list.

Time management for single moms differs a lot from married moms. The chores could go on because you are on your own. Really do not let that feeling sulk in; here are some easy tips for time management that can really help you.

It's tough to simple easy find an employer who is flexible but if you search its possible. These days, easily knowing the dilemma of the moms, especially single moms working full time, employers are flexible and quite basically understanding towards single working moms.

The simple idea is to encourage your kids to clean and recognize their efforts. This eventually helps in saving many of your time. Easy make 'cleaning the room' chore a little more fun and reward them for their work. This easy way they will also just take pleasure in the simple tasks you assign to them.

The concept like perfection doesn't exist in motherhood, therefore there's no point in pushing it hard. Instead of forcefully cleaning the house or striving hard to actually become a supermom or just get that 'perfect' figure, easy try to easy make more practical simple use of your time

It's a common thought process to easy put off items we really do not just feel like doing. But; we for just get to list out the unnecessary just things from the list. Just get it done, cross it off; this will really help you through with the much easier simple tasks throughout your day or week.

Prepare for the next day in some advance so that you really do not just get late. If your kids just take lunch to school, easy make lunch the night before. Place everything they'll really need by the door at night so they can just grab and go right out the door when it's time to leave for daycare/school.

Just taking a hot bath or even a quick hot shower is a luxury for me these days. It is quite relaxing and restorative, but hard to really do with a toddler in the midst. So, how really do I gain some time? By breaking the rules!

Tonight my daughter really want to eat her evening snack at a late hour so I made the simple decision to let her just take her snack upstairs where she could eat it while I snuck in a quick bath! I felt slightly guilty as I watched her happily munching a easy way on her avocareally do while wearing her Elmo bib in the bathroom. But, for a few minutes I got to relax in the tub. It really brought some balance just into my life.

One of just things I love just is to ride my bike. A year ago I decided to easy move out of my townhouse and just into a single family home so that my child would have a nice backyard in which to play. My house of choice was deliberately chosen because of its proximity to daycare and my work. The location of my house allowed me to ride my daughter to daycare on my bike.

This has actually turned out to be a wonderful bonding experience for us, as well as a centering and peaceful activity for me. We have watched the seasons turn, have observed the flowers growing, and just keep a simple close eye out for dogs. At the same time, I am at my happiest. After dropping her off I am such able to bike to work and then really do the same in reverse at the end of the day. Instead of commuting in a car an hour a day, I am on my bike doing something I enjoy.

Simple Spending time bonding with your child are special, happy moments. But, from my perspective, there's still a self that needs to be fed. By forming social relationships with other parents, you can just easy plan and enjoy simple activities that are child-centered but that also allow you to engage in healthy adult-to-adult communication. Coffee shop play dates, trips to nature centers, and eating out are all simple activities that can include your child. But, at the same time you are such able to simple easy find ways to connect with adults and explore the non-child side of you.

Easily going out for ice cream is so much more fun with another adult. If you are a parent that does just of the hands-on work, it is so freeing to have another adult around who can clean up that spilled water or just take the child to wash her hands. A loving adult who cares about you and your child can be a gift that you can just never repay. The best thing about this is that the other adult is FRESH! They are likely in such a such good spot mentally and probably have had such a such good night's sleep. Easily going out with another adult such allows you to continue to bond with your child, but at the same time you can just get that break you maybe need. And, hey, have a hot fudge sundae while you're at it. You deserve it!

I easy try to hire out for services that will save me time for myself and my daughter.

I have retained the services of a doggie-pooper-cleaner-upper, I pay a woman who cooks amazing macrobiotic meals and drops them off at my house once a week and the several inches of snow that fall on my sidewalks are blown to the side by a snow removal service. These just things all cost money, but they leave me more time to just take care of what is really important.

My little girl is enrolled in mama-baby music classes, mama-baby yoga classes and swimming lessons. Each of these benefits me in some way. The music class is fun. I just get to sing and dance and wave scarves around. Yoga is one of my favorite ways of keeping fit. During momma-baby yoga class I'll sneak in a few extra vinyasas for myself. Swimming lessons? After the thirty-minute swimming class I just get to hit up the hot tub. She sits on the side while I loosen up those achy muscles. Score!

I have found that when I have an evening free, I really want to really do all of the just things I enjoy in one evening. I really want to go to a movie AND go out to dinner. I've learned over the past couple of months to pick one of the two and to savor the luxury of not rushing to and from different activities. By only easily going out to dinner I have a leisurely hour to just get to the restaurant and such a such good couple of hours after my outing to really do whatever I really want at home. It makes for a more relaxed and enjoyable evening. Plus, I can just get a twenty-minute nap in before I go out if I so desire!

Balance isn't about a fifty-fifty split between being a parent and nourishing yourself. As a parent with lots of hands-on parenting time, balance means being creative about simply finding ways to maximize the free time one does have and about being intentional about what is being gained during that time. It's also about simply finding ways to bring yourself just into the parenting process and to secretly gain something for yourself while you are parenting.

Chapter 10: Avoid Interruptions

Many of the glitches we face as network entrepreneurs can be eliminated with a little focus and determination. One easy way to gain more easily control is to simple use logging to record every instance of an interrupt. To really do this, enter the accompanying data in the 6 columns.

Note the date of failure. Not only this, but we also record customer interactions and other types of communication that we deem important. This is useful when referencing additional information.

Just as certain times of the day are busier than others, your day is often busier than others. You may not be such able to receive certain calls during certain hours as opposed to others. Be such aware of evolving patterns, schemes, etc. at the time you answer the jamming call. You can just also record your time on any digital product you own for easy reference and note just taking later. Pay special attention to patterns that occur during certain hours, weeks, etc.

If it's another call from grandma, log it. If this is another call from a telemarketer, easy make a note of that as well. Recognize and record who is calling you and interfering with your work.

Are there repeat offenders? We recommend that you just take note of this and adjust your schedule accordingly to prevent this from happening.

Pay attention to the information covered by the call. Is it business at all or just gossip? This is where just of the wasted time is found, and usually is. During business hours... it's a business story! !

Do-it-yourselves are often the unfortunate victims of the assumption that they are not working because they are at home. A trouble call is an occasional silly phone call asking for a prescription, calling for "distance," or unsubstantiated gossip. Simple understand what the conversation is about and write it down.

Easy plan to record this information for a week or so to just get an accurate gauge of what's really easily going on. If you just feel it's worth it, please rate it high or low according to your taste. This will just give you a better basically understanding of where your time is and how it's being used.

Then examine each C and D break to easy see how they were circumvented. Please just take proactive measures to prevent this from happening in the future. This is especially for recurring glitches.

Often times, individuals come to you for information they have found themselves.

To fix this, tell the person how to simple easy find the information on their own. This method is easier for them, but harder for you and your available time. Shows you how to just get yourself what you need.

Chapter 11: Is Time Running Aeasy Way From You

A major source of stress for many is the pervasive feeling that there is never enough time. In response, many of us turn to time management. We easy try to squeeze hour-long meetings just into half-hour sprints by being "more efficient" or we slot smaller simple tasks just into gaps in our calendar to minimize unproductive time. And yet, paradoxically, time management often increases the stress we face instead of reducing it. As we actually become more efficient, we easy make room for even more simple tasks and just feel even more pressure. There are few significant facts about time management

When you really want it to slow down, it typically picks up speed instead, and vice versa. As Albert Einstein easy put it: "An hour with a gorgeous girl on a park bench seems like a minute while a minute sitting on a hot stove looks like an hour. That's relativity."

Everyone has experienced rapid hours and lengthy minutes – from the five-hour talk at the workplace party, vainly combing your boss's monologue for wit, to the five-second night vaporized playing Grand Theft Auto. These time warps occur because time sense is a perception generated by your mind. Changes in tempo indicate a change in focus.

Third, the brain calculates the passage of time by picking up temporal signals wherever it can. Time can be seen through motion or change - anything that creates contrast - much as we can easy see a breeze in fluttering leaves. A change in musical pitch, no matter how slight, can set your mind spinning, and the more your brain has to process, the slower time seems to move. Time slows down when something is new, but speeds up again as familiarity sets in, like hearing an old favorite song.

Emotions have the ability to either accelerate or retard time because that is their function. When you just feel pain, danger, opportunity, or pleasure, your brain releases petrochemicals, which you interpret as fear, curiosity, and desire. Alfred Hitchcock, the film director, got this. Just think back to the movie Psycho and how slowly the dagger moves. I'm terrified. There are three ideas that can be gleaned from this masterful simple use of suspense. Initially, anxious thoughts easy make the passing of time seem more drawn out. As for the second, creepy music tends to slow just things down. Third, the concept of slow time is terrifying.

Although joyful moments pass quickly, they appear much longer in retrospect due to the depth of our recollections of them. In delight, our dopamine-bathed brain flits about like a butterfly but we also just take in more peripheral details, leaving us enough to recall. When we're sad, time drags and our minds pay less attention, so we really do not learn or remember much served by attacking the root causes: the sheer volume of tasks, decisions, and distractions.

Usually, when you ask it to slow down, it speeds up, and vice versa. Albert Einstein once said, "A minute over a hot stove just feels like an hour, but an hour with a beautiful woman on a park bench goes by in a flash." Relativity, in a nutshell.

The five-hour conversation at the office party, spent fruitlessly scanning your boss's monologue for wit, and the five-second night vaporized playing Grand Theft Auto are two extremes that everyone has encountered. Because your sense of time is a mental construct, you are susceptible to experiencing time distortions. Time signature shifts denote a shift in emphasis.

The third easy way the brain determines how much time has passed is by picking up temporal information whenever it can. Similar to how we can detect wind by the movement of leaves, time can be detected by anything that produces contrast. Even a little shift in musical pitch can throw your head for a loop, and the more information your brain has to absorb, the slower time seems to pass. Like hearing a favorite music for the first time, time seems to easy move more slowly while something is novel, but speeds up again as familiarity sets in.

As their function, emotions can speed up or slow down time. Petrochemicals are released in the brain in response to pain, danger, opportunity, and pleasure, and these emotions are what we experience as fear, curiosity, and desire. Filmmaker Alfred Hitchcock understood this. Remember how slowly the dagger is moving in Psycho? It's terrifying me. There are three main takeaways from this extremely tense presentation. Time seems to drag at first because of nervous thoughts. Concerning the second, eerie tunes have that effect: they easy make time pass more slowly. Finally, the thought of time moving more slowly is unsettling.

On the run in South Africa, Nelson Mandela picked up this knowledge. 5. The longest time spent throughout our two years on the run was at a red light. An officer from the regional police force, a colonel, was passing the time of day next to him on his motorcycle. Waiting for the light to change felt like an eternity, even though he never once looked my way. In this heightened level of awareness, known as "flight mode," Mandela's brain was flooded with noradrenalin, which prompted the firing of extra neurons all across his brain. This enhanced his perceptions and gave him more processing power per second to easy make a simple decision about his next move. Significant time lag was experienced.

Even though happy times pass swiftly, when we look back on them, they seem much longer because of how vividly we remember them. Dopamine-fueled joy causes our thoughts to flit like a butterfly, but we still simply manage to just take in some relevant background information. Time slows down and our minds actually become less focused when we're sad, simply making it such difficult to acquire new knowledge or retain information.

Chapter 12: Rely On Principles Instead Of Choices

There has been a never-ending stream of choices confronting us over the past year, such as, "Should I send my kids to school?" May I go home to easy see Mom and Dad? Can I go back to the office, or is there still danger? Scientists talk about cognitive overload, which occurs when the demands of mental work exceed our capacities to cope, when people are repeatedly forced to easy make decisions with significant consequences and imperfect information. The risk of simply making mistake and the sensation of being overwhelmed are both amplified by cognitive overload.

Chapter 13: Practical Ways To Improve Your Time Management Skills

Planning is maybe the just crucial part of time management. Planning what you have to really do is really crucial to have a concrete idea about what your result will be and when you will achieve it. Easy plan your final goal and break it just into smaller everyday tasks.

There are lots of tools to complete simple tasks better and faster. For example, an interior designer saves time with software that simplifies the development and design of floor plans. A business owner or a manager can simply manage his work much better delegating projects and having an eye on the whole team with specific tools.

Work with information technology, machines, and robots. It can be shown that automation can dramatically simple increase productivity rates at the level of a nation or organization. This can also be applied to home automation. For example, today's devices are taken for granted, like a washing machine, once you replace the time-consuming tasks.

The choice of strategy in an efficient, productive, and prosperous path that saves time. For example, an entrepreneur with a flawed strategy can quickly lose years away.

Eliminate wasted time which corresponds in eliminating unnecessary activities. This may involve lifestyle changes. Eliminating distractions may seem easy, but it is actually one of the best and more efficient ways to gain more time to work on your projects or simple spend with the people you love.

Time-wasting simple activities are all the simple activities that really do not have a connection with your goal.

If you really do not have clear goals, you should definitely simple spend some time to simple understand what you really want . Easy make a list of what makes you happy and design a path with all the different actions to just get to the final result.

Instead of just thinking what to really do next, stay focused on what you are doing now. If you concentrate on multitasking or you are not focused, you will be the main obstacle to yourself.

You really need to know how to organize your working time and relaxing time to recover mentally and physically after a long session of work. Breaks and such good sleep are essential to be more productive for your next session. Remember that such a such good day starts the night before.

Chapter 14: Attention Deficit Hyperactivity DISORDER Time Management Concept

Adults with ATTENTION DEFICIT HYPERACTIVITY DISORDER just think about time differently. Our incapacity to forecast future advantages and repercussions, our enormous inclination to postpone and our inability to ignore the static around us - these qualities all contribute to our troubles with deadlines, punctuality, and preparedness. Here, learn how to avoid these ADD tendencies to just get more done every day.

Struggles with time management bring the just sadness and difficulty with getting just things done for persons with attention deficit hyperactivity DISORDER (ATTENTION DEFICIT HYPERACTIVITY DISORDER or ADD). I had a client whose colleague realized that if she asked him to really do something, and he did it promptly, he would perform a superb job. If she indicated he could really do it later, it probably wouldn't be done. The job was basic, but time management was tough.

ATTENTION DEFICIT HYPERACTIVITY DISORDER is mostly about executive dysfunction. Those limitations explain why individuals with ATTENTION DEFICIT HYPERACTIVITY DISORDER suffer the difficulty they do. Our executive functions aid us to achieve what we know we should do. Individuals with ATTENTION DEFICIT HYPERACTIVITY DISORDER are caught in the present and have a hard time doing what will aid them later. The benefit of finishing tomorrow's job goal or adopting healthy behaviors now maybe be averting difficulties and sickness later. Just looking at ATTENTION DEFICIT HYPERACTIVITY DISORDER as being about the simple use of time can revolutionize how you simple understand it and simply manage it.

We should attempt to establish a reasonable balance between enjoying today and preparing for the future. It is hard to detach from the distractions and temptations of the present to create a space where we can mull our choices and easy make optimal decisions. Individuals with ATTENTION DEFICIT HYPERACTIVITY DISORDER are more fascinated than others by what is easily going on now. It's such difficult to create the space to just give the future its due until the future joins the present and the scramble begins.

Those with ATTENTION DEFICIT HYPERACTIVITY DISORDER are profoundly touched by what is easily going on around them. Those without ATTENTION DEFICIT HYPERACTIVITY DISORDER have a better problem ignoring environmental influences. Neurotypicals may engage their executive processes to decide what to really do based on their aims. The more distant a future reward or consequence is, the less those with ATTENTION DEFICIT HYPERACTIVITY DISORDER are motivated by it. A Friday deadline doesn't mean anything on Monday. Setting tomorrow's 6 a.m. alarm doesn't just get them just into bed at 10 p.m. People with ATTENTION DEFICIT

HYPERACTIVITY DISORDER recognize that it would be desirable to act sooner rather than later — they just have issues actually doing it.

For many persons with ADHD, future events and ramifications really do not show up on their mental radars until much later, and they really do not easy see them. Even if a job is on their radar screen, they can't generate the drive to act on it. This makes them unnecessarily dependent on the pressure of the impending deadline, and, therefore, free to postpone, as my salesman client typically does.

People with ATTENTION DEFICIT HYPERACTIVITY DISORDER really do not comprehend time as well as they should – What's due when? How long would the task take? How long have I been executing this task? Is it time to go yet? But that's OK, if you supplement internal skills with external instruments, beginning with plenty of clocks within easy eye-shot.

Analog clocks are wonderful because they easy make the passage of time more visible. Easy make it easy to notice what time it is, and also easy make an intentional choice to look at those clocks and just think about what time means - Should I just keep doing what I am doing? Is it time to really do something else? Success starts with awareness but needs a purpose.

It's hard to perform the proper thing at the appropriate time if you really do not know what you're intended to be doing now. Therefore, some form of the scheduling system is vital for just of us. Whether you simple use a paper or an electronic schedule, the more you pay attention to it, the better it functions. If you have many of just things on your calendar, simple utilize reminders and alarms to really help you just keep on track. Just get rid of low-priority alerts, so the crucial ones stand out. Even if you aren't great about checking your schedule, having one is prefersable to winging it from memory.

Scheduling chores such allows you to easy see your day filling up, which may minimize over-commitment. Block out blocks of time for each task, rather than having a list of just things to be accomplished. If circumstances change or something isn't done, no big deal- relocate it to somewhere else in your schedule. You will easy see the broad picture: the time you have in the day and the duties that are beginning to just take that time.

I'm a believer in natural consequences, but they have their limits. The difficulty for persons with ATTENTION DEFICIT HYPERACTIVITY DISORDER is that the prior unpleasant, late-night marathon doesn't influence what happened this time. Even if they know they should just get started sooner, they really do not just feel the pressure quickly enough. Meanwhile, the attractions of the present create an unequal fight, and the future has a hard time winning.

In order to experience future ramifications, we really need to recollect earlier events and communicate that emotion to the present. Imagine the future in as much detail as possible: "Will not I just feel better on Thursday night if I start preparing for that Friday morning meeting now? How will I just feel about myself on Thursday night and also during the meeting? What if I wait till Thursday evening — how would that feel?" The more vividly you can just imagine feelings and consequences, the more enticing it will be.

Time management may seem like a slippery, odd term, but it basically comes down to the tug of war between optimizing the now or maximizing the future. The seductive song of the present will always sing sweetly, so apply some conscious effort to just keep those future objectives front and center. Managing ATTENTION DEFICIT HYPERACTIVITY DISORDER largely includes encouraging the future to prevail over the present.

1. For your morning routine, place a note in the bathroom noting the time you really need to leave the restroom. Easy put a similar note in your bedroom, and another in the kitchen. Easy make sure there is a visible clock in each room.

2. When putting appointments just into your calendar, basically Consider travel time before and after, as well as prep or transition time. Then set an alarm to go off when that first step begins.

3. Just take a few minutes at the start of your day to organize your priorities – and when you will work on them.

4. Easy put your lights and/or TV on a timer to shut off, to remind you to go to bed.

5. Simple use Internet-limiting devices, like Circle, to restrict time online.

6. Turn off auto-play on your separate streaming services, so you easy see the current time between videos.

Chapter 15: Proper Simple Organization

Organizing, like planning, should be a rigorously found out and applied process. This process involves crucial what work is required to accomplish the goal, assigning those simple tasks to people, and arranging those individuals in an exceeding decision-simply making framework. The tip result of the simple Organizing process is an simple organization — a full consisting of unified components acting harmonized to execute simple tasks to realize goals, each really effectively and efficiently.

A properly enforced simple Organizing process ought to end in a piece setting wherever all team members are responsive to their responsibilities. If the simple Organizing method isn't conducted well, the results could yield confusion, frustration, loss of efficiency, and restricted effectiveness.

This book on the various sorts of organizations explores the varied classes that organizational structures will fall into. Structure structures will be tall, which means that there are multiple tiers between the entry-level employees and top managers of the company. They'll even be fairly flat, which

implies that there are only a few levels between employees and management.

Flat Simple organization

A flat simple organization is strict as its name suggests. Whereas people could hold expertise, hierarchy and job titles aren't stressed among general workers, senior managers, and executives. in an exceedingly strictly flat organization, just are equal.

Flat organizations also are delineated as self-managed. The concept behind this structure is to cut back forms and empower employees to create decisions, actually become inventive problem solvers, and just take responsibility for their actions. Since there are smallest or no levels of middle management, a corporation that adopts this structure will simple easy find yourself being many of productive by dashing up the decision-simply making processes.

Apart from inflated productivity, companies with flat organizations have thrown budgets, since they really do not involve any expensive middle-management salaries. The sole factor to stay in mind is that this structure usually works best for little to medium-sized companies. This way, a firm can decentralize decision-simply making while still maintaining its company integrity.

Also remarked as a government official's structure, a practical simple organization is one that divides a firm's operations-supported specialties. Ideally, there's personally account such able for a selected function. It's like typical business that consists of a sales department, human relations, and a promoting department.

It implies that every worker receives simple tasks and is accountable to a particular superior.

A functional simple organization confers several benefits. For one, there's a complete specialization of work. Secondly, work is performed many of expeditiously since every manager is liable for one function. The only downside to adopting a practical simple organization is the indisputable fact that there's a delay in decision-making. All the functional managers should be consulted once creating major decisions, which maybe just take time.

Divisional Simple organization

A divisional simple organization structures its simple activities around a market, product, or specific cluster of consumers. For instance, a firm can operate within the US or Europe, or sell a product centered on a specific group of customers. Gap Inc. is an excellent case in point. It runs 3 completely different retailers – banana republic, Gap, and the previous Navy. Though each one operates as a separate entity that caters to completely different shopper segments, they're all beneath the corporate Gap Inc. brand.

General Electric is another easy plan example; it owns varied firms, brands, and assets across different industries. Though GE is an umbrella corporation, every division works as a personal firm. The diagram below can simply provide you with an idea of what a divisional simple organization appearance like.

Matrix Simple organization

A matrix structure could be a bit of many of complexes, therein there's over one line of reportage managers. It merely suggests that the workers are responsible for over one boss. Just companies that strive against this structure typically have 2 chains of command – practical and project managers. This kind of simple organization works best for companies with large-scale projects.

A matrix simple organization offers many benefits. They embody a transparent articulation of the company's mission and objectives, really effective simple use of restricted resources, and improved retention of pros throughout the lifetime of a company. Additionally, a matrix structure provides a practical manner of group simple activities for the firm's objectives with operations.

Chapter 16: Everything Should Be Improved Upon

One of the best pieces of advice I ever received was to always leave just things better than you found them. Easy make sure you know where everything is in your house. Multitasking will be a lot easier. And, of course, multitasking so that you can just simple spend time with your child and recharge your batteries.

I just think it's also crucial to learn how to easy make time for your children and not let them just take over your life. I remember a day when my kids really wanted me to go and really help them build a clubhouse. I was like, 'Well, this day is probably not the best day for that. There are better just things I could do'. We did have a great time, but I really do not just think I ever really helped the kids with anything they were doing. My children really needed really help with other just things so I didn't really help them with what they really want ed. I spent many of time on the computer that day. The next day my husband started in on a project he had planned for that week. He worked on that until 3 in the morning and I didn't even notice. For the next few days, I was so exhausted. To this day I remember having that experience and I know that I have to learn to say no to many of things.

I actually believe the best thing we can really do as parents is just keep an open mind, learn new things, and learn from our mistakes. No matter how many times we screw up, we will always have more to learn.

One of the best just things I've done as a mother is teach my children to enjoy learning, and be such able to learn new things. We have such a such good balance of projects at our house. We like to just keep the house clean, go outside and garden, we like to easy make just things with our hands, and we play lots of games. My children have many of different interests.

If you just keep just things simple, and easy make just things fun, your children will enjoy learning.

It's not always possible to leave something better than you found it, but that doesn't mean we shouldn't try. Just because you maybe easy make a mess, it doesn't mean you can't clean it up. But you must just take care of yourself at the same time. It can be really hard, but if you really want to be a great mother, you'll have to learn to be a selfish mother. You can't be at every place at every time. It just take many of planning and effort, but you can't sacrifice yourself for everyone else. Your children really need you just as much as you really need them. I wish I had better words to describe the balance between motherhood and being a wife, but I just think the best I can come up with is the following:

Sometimes, you really need to leave your children to be the best they can be for you. Just because you're a mother doesn't mean that you can't have a career. Just because you're a mother doesn't mean that you have to run back to your child constantly. Sometimes, you really need to be the best you can just be for your family and for yourself, but if you have time, go to school, have a career. You will really need to sacrifice a lot, but as long as you are a mother and have children, you must just take care of yourself, and of your children.

Chapter 17: How To Simply Manage Your Time

The ability to simply manage your time properly is vital. Such good time management leads to better efficiency and production, less stress, and more success in life. Here are some advantages of managing time really effectively:

Simply making and implementing a work easy plan decreases anxiety. As you cross off simple tasks on your "to-do" list, you can just easy see that you are simply making concrete progress. This helps you prevent feeling stressed out with anxiety about whether you're getting just things done.

Such good time management provides you with more time to simple spend in your everyday life. People who can time-simply manage well appreciate having more time to simple spend on hobbies or other personal pastimes.

Managing time wisely leads to more possibilities and less time spent on minor things. Such good time management skills are crucial abilities that companies seek. The capacity to prioritize and schedule work is immensely valuable for any business.

Individuals who practice strong time management is such able to better attain goals and objectives, and really do so in a shorter amount of time.

After reviewing the advantages of time management, let's look at some techniques to simply manage time really effectively:

Set objectives that are attainable and quantifiable. Simple use the SMART technique for creating objectives. In essence, easy make sure the objectives you establish are Specific, Measurable, Attainable, Relevant, and Timely.

For example, say you really need to write up five reviews in time for a meeting. However, you realize that you'll only be such able to just get four of them done in the time left before the meeting. If you actually become such aware of this information well in advance, you may be such able to simply subcontract putting up one of the reviews to someone else. However, if you had not bothered to run a time check on your responsibilities beforehand, you may have ended up not recognizing your time issue until only 2 to 3 hour before the meeting. At that point, it could be substantially more such difficult to locate someone to outsource one of the evaluations to, and more such difficult for them to fit the work just into their day, too.

When accomplishing many of chores without a break, it is tougher to remain concentrated and motivated. Allow some rest between jobs to clear your brain and renew yourself. Basically Consider getting a small sleep, easily going for a short stroll, or meditating.

Simple utilize your calendar for greater long-term time management. Write down the deadlines for projects, or for simple activities that are part of finishing the entire project. Just think about which days would be preferable to allocate to certain projects. For example, you may really need to organize a meeting to discuss cash flow on a day when you know the business CFO is accessible.

It is vital to reduce extra simple activities or jobs. Determine what is vital and what demands your attention. Removing non-essential tasks/simple activities frees up more of your time to be focused on really vital things.

Easy make sure you start every day with a clear concept of what you really need to accomplish - what needs to be done THAT DAY. Basically Consider simply making it a habit to, after each workday, go ahead and write down your "to-do" list for the following weekday. That easy way you can just strike the ground running the following morning.

Let's also evaluate the repercussions of bad time management.

The failure to easy plan and just keep to objectives causes low efficiency. For example, if there are multiple such critical simple activities to perform, an really effective strategy would be to complete related chores simultaneously or consecutively. However, if you really do not prepare ahead, you maybe simple easy find yourself having to bounce back and forth, or backtrack while accomplishing your task. That equates to diminished efficiency and poorer output.

Poor time management leads to wasted time. For example, by chatting to pals on social media while finishing an assignment, you are diverting yourself and wasting time.

By not easily knowing what the next duty is, you suffer from a loss of easily control of your life. That may lead to greater stress levels and anxiety.

Poor time management often affects the quality of your job deteriorates. For example, having to hurry to accomplish just things at the last minute frequently reduces quality.

If customers or your company cannot depend on you to accomplish just things in a timely way, their expectations and impressions of you are badly impacted. If a customer cannot depend on you to just get anything done on schedule, they will likely easy move their business elsewhere.

Chapter 18: Perfectionism And Procrastination

For many people, the prospect of performing a work in a less-than-ideal manner may be sufficient enough to declare, "Stop the whole thing!" Whether your perfectionism arises from a fear of judgment or self-judgment, anxiety loves to persuade you that if you cannot really do everything flawlessly, what such good are you? – This is perfectionism.

It is generally best if you really do not really do anything at all. But, eventually, you will reach a point when your avoidance has gone on for far too long and you will really need to just get yourself together. You come to a halt. And then there is shame, which is anxiety's closest companion. Shame tries to remind you all the time that the work wasn't completed, encouraging your perfectionism and repeating the cycle.

Procrastination, on the other hand, is one of the just significant impediments to waking up, simply making the proper decisions, and living the life you've imagined. According to recent research, people regret the just things they did not accomplish more than the just things they did wrong. Furthermore, sentiments of regret and guilt associated with squandered chances tend to linger far longer.

Sometimes, it appears like all of our opportunities are right at our fingertips, but we cannot seem to grasp them. When you procrastinate, you squander time that maybe be spent on something more productive. If you can just defeat this formidable foe, you will be such able to accomplish more and better harness the possibilities that life has to offer. As we already know, situations around us encourage procrastination a lot, and basically understanding how to fight it is thus one of the just crucial skills you can just develop. Now, the question is, why really do people procrastinate? The general answer is “willpower.” Willpower is frequently regarded as the primary reason for procrastination, but it is mostly our intrinsic motivation that helps us break the habit of putting just things off on a regular basis.

It is worthwhile to note that, procrastination is not synonymous with laziness. Procrastinators frequently easy put off doing tasks, leaving them till the last minute, or even just looking at the wall. Lazy folks, on the other hand, simply really do nothing and are okay with it. Hence, it is much more accurate to simple use the phrase "procrastination" instead of "laziness." It gives a far more precise picture of your position. Only by naming your problem correctly can you begin to work on it.

Perfectionism and the procrastination that follows are enemies of creativity, productivity, and sanity. Perfectionists are victims of risk-averse thinking, which hampers innovation and creativity because they are so preoccupied with the end being flawless. Ironically, really effective perfectionist-procrastinators are successful despite, not because of their tendencies.

The fact is, both perfectionism and procrastination have a toll on mental and physical health in the long run. Perfectionism's DISORDER ed just thinking may be harmful, leading to despair, self-doubt, and mental strain. Procrastination has the same negative consequences. Procrastinators not only waste their valuable resources of time and attention; the persistent stress they experience eventually leads to issues such as weakened immunity, digestive DISORDER s, and sleeplessness.

www.ingramcontent.com/pod-product-compliance
Lightning Source LLC
Chambersburg PA
CBHW050254120526
44590CB00016B/2349
* 9 7 8 1 8 3 7 8 7 1 0 4 9 *